John Douglas

A Letter Addressed to Two Great Men, on the Prospect of

Peace

And on the terms necessary to be insisted upon in the negociation

John Douglas

A Letter Addressed to Two Great Men, on the Prospect of Peace
And on the terms necessary to be insisted upon in the negociation

ISBN/EAN: 9783337075248

Printed in Europe, USA, Canada, Australia, Japan

Cover: Foto ©ninafisch / pixelio.de

More available books at **www.hansebooks.com**

A

LETTER

ADDRESSED TO

Two GREAT MEN.

[Price One Shilling.]

A LETTER

Two GREAT MEN,

ON THE

PROSPECT of PEACE;

And on the TERMS necessary to be insisted upon in the NEGOCIATION.

Mea quidem sententiâ, paci, quæ nihil habitura sit insidiarum, semper est consulendum. De Offic. Lib. 1.

There is a Tide in the Affairs of Men,
Which taken at the Flood, leads on to Fortune;
Omitted, all the Voyage of their Life
Is bound in Shallows and in Miseries.
On such a full Sea are we now a-float,
And we must take the Current when it serves,
Or lose our Ventures. SHAKESP.

Printed for A. MILLAR, in the Strand.
MDCCLX.

A

LETTER

Addressed to

Two GREAT MEN.

My Lord, *and* Sir,

YOU will be furprized at an Addrefs made to you jointly in this Manner; but as I have not the Honour to be much acquainted with either of you, (though I efteem you both, at leaft while you remain connected) I hope you will forgive me for troubling you, in this public Way; and the rather, as as I think the Matters I fhall write upon, to be of very great Importance; and as you will difcover by what I am going to fuggeft to you, that I am a true Friend to Old *England*, and a fincere Lover of my Country.

I have long thought that our *Minifters of State* may be much affifted, in their Deliberations, by Perfons who have not the Honour of fitting at the Council-board. The wifeft Meafures have often

B been

been pointed out, in the Courſe of parliamentary Debate; and Members of either Houſe, perhaps thoſe leaſt conſulted by Government, have frequently been earlieſt in ſuggeſting ſuch Plans of public Policy, as Government itſelf has been glad to adopt. The Extinction of factious Oppoſition, the Unanimity of every Party, and the Acquieſcence of every Connection, in whatever Scheme is propoſed by his Majeſty's Servants, while it hath produced infinite Advantages to the Public; hath deprived thoſe who direct the Cabinet, of all ſuch Parliamentary Inſtruction, as their Predeceſſors in Power uſed to receive. You, my Lord, of late, ſcarcely hear any Speech in the Houſe of Lords, but that of a Lawyer on a *Scotch* Appeal; and the hereditary Council of the Nation rarely aſſemble for higher Purpoſes than to alter *Settlements* and deliberate on Bills of *Divorce*. And you, Sir, in the other Houſe, where ſo many ſkillful Champions uſed formerly to engage, and ſtruggle for Victory, remain ſingle in the Field of Battle; and your Speaker takes the Chair only to vote *Millions* and levy Thouſands, without the leaſt Debate or Oppoſition.

The Channel of Parliamentary Inſtruction being thus ſtopt, no other but that of the Preſs is left open, for thoſe Heads of Advice to which it may be worth your while to attend. For this Reaſon it is, that I have thought of addreſſing you in this Manner. Who I am, it matters not. Let it ſuffice, that, unpenſioned and unemployed, I can vie, in Zeal for the Public, with thoſe who taſte the Sweets of exorbitant Salaries, and unfathomed Perquiſites. Whether my Knowledge be equal to my Zeal; whether my Acquaintance with the World, and Experience in Buſineſs, have enabled me to offer any Thing that may be of real Utility, muſt

be

be determined by you, and by the Public. This I am certain of, that my Intention is honeft; and while I pleafe myfelf, I fhall endeavour, at the fame time, not to offend either of you. Some Productions, in which you have, of late, been jointly taken Notice of, proceeded from a *factious* Difpofition, which I am unacquainted with, and deteft. For, far from wifhing to difunite and feparate your Interefts, I am fully perfuaded that without your perfect Harmony and Union, the great Events which have happened under your Adminiftration, will not have thofe permanent good Confequences fo much to be wifhed for: And it is only from your joint Concurrence, that we can hope for any of thofe prudent, fpirited and national Meafures concerning which I propofe to offer you a few Hints, in this Addrefs.

Confidering the prefent diftreffed Condition of *France*, fallen from its alarming Power, and Greatnefs, into the loweft State of Diftrefs and Impotence; unfortunate in its military Operations in every Quarter of the Globe; beaten all *Europe* over by Sea and Land; its Fleets failing, only to be deftroyed; its Armies marching, only to run away; without Trade; no Credit; ftopping Payments, protefting Bills, and to all Intents and Purpofes a Bankrupt Nation; their King, the Princes of the Blood, the Nobility, and the Clergy carrying in all their Plate to be coined, for the prefent extreme Exigency of their Affairs; difappointed and baffled in all their Schemes on the Continent, and taught to think no more of *Invafions*, by the Deftruction of the only Fleet they had left; — I fay, confidering all thefe Circumftances, which I have not exaggerated, in the leaft, it is not unnatural to imagine, that a Period will foon be put to the Troubles of *Europe*. *France*, unable to carry on the War, muft

foon

soon be reduced to the Neceffity of fuing for Peace.

We have had Bloodfhed enough. God forgive thofe who have occafioned this terrible Deftruction of the human Species, and fpread Mifery, and Devaftation, for fo long a Time, in almoft every Corner of the Globe. The great Succefs with which the Arms of *Britain* have been bleffed, puts it in our Power to give Peace to *Europe:* and it is to the Honour of his Majefty and thofe who direct his Councils, that the Diftreffes of our Enemies have only enabled him to give the World a Proof of his Moderation; and to fhew that his Inclination to make Peace, keeps Pace with the Inability of *France* to prolong the War.

" As his Majefty entered into this War, not " from Views of Ambition, fo he does not wifh " to continue it, from Motives of Refentment. " The Defire of his Majefty's Heart is, to fee a " Stop put to the Effufion of Chriftian Blood."

What was declared, in the above Paragraph of his Majefty's Speech from the Throne, to our own Parliament, at the Opening of this Seffion, has fince that, been notified in Form to our Enemy. The Readinefs of *England*, and *Pruffia*, to enter into a Treaty, and to give Peace to Chriftendom, which Prince *Lewis* of *Wolfenbuttle* hath been authorized to communicate to the *French* Minifter at the *Hague*, will, no doubt, open the Door for a Negociation, in a Manner the moft likely to be embraced by the Court of *Verfailles*; whofe Difgraces and Diftreffes too great to be diffembled, and too extenfive to be remedied, will difpofe them to liften with Attention to every propofal of Accommodation, made to them by an Enemy whofe Sword was unfheathed only to punifh Perfidy; and whofe Succeffes, as appears from their making the firft Advances

towards

towards a Treaty, have not infatuated them to prefer unneceffary and ruinous Conqueft, to a reafonable and folid Peace.

It is, therefore, to be hoped, and to be believed, that Peace is not at a great Diftance; and upon this Suppofition I fhall beg Leave to offer a few Confiderations to *you*, as to the Perfons on whom the Fate of this Country depends; Confiderations which are equally important as they are feafonable; and an Attention to which, before you enter upon any Negociation, may, perhaps, affift you (if I may be allowed to fuppofe you ftand in Need of any Affiftance) in directing this Negociation to fuch an Iffue, as may be equally honourable to yourfelves, and ufeful to the Public.

In this Situation of Affairs, one of the firft Matters relative to the future Negociation, which, no doubt, muft occur to you, will be, the Choice of thofe Perfons who are to be trufted with the great Concerns of this Nation as *Plenipotentiaries.* And, as much will depend upon this Point, I fhall beg Leave to begin with giving you my Thoughts upon it, and the other Topics on which I propofe to trouble you will naturally arife from each other without obferving any other *Order,* or Connection, befides that in which they fhall prefent themfelves to a Mind intent upon its Subject.

With regard then, to the Choice of *Plenipotentiaries,* I cannot but lament the Difficulties you have to encounter, before you will be able to find fuch as the Public will have Reafon to thank you for. — I am not totally unknowing in the Characters and Capacities of many among the great. But when I caft my Eyes around me, I own that I am furprized, greatly furprized, but ftill more grieved, to find fo few among us, capable of conducting the arduous Tafk of making a Peace. Whether this

4

hath

hath arifen from Negleƈt in the Education of our Men of Quality; or whether the Qualifications which fit them for Statefmen, have been negleƈted, in Comparifon of fuch as fit them for *Arthur*'s or *Newmarket*; or whether it be owing to the State Policy fo fyftematically adopted, of late Years, of giving Places, not to the Perfons who can beft execute the Bufinefs—but to thofe who can beft do a Job. Whatever be the Caufe, the Faƈt is certain; and it is Matter of Amazement that there fhould be fo few in this Ifland, who have given any Proofs that they are capable of conduƈting with Ability, much lefs with Dexterity, this important Bufinefs of a Negociation with *France*. Men who are verfed in Treaties, knowing the Interefts, Pretenfions, and Connexions of the feveral Princes of *Europe*; fkilled in the Principles of public Law, and capable of applying them on every particular Occafion; acquainted with the Commerce, the Colonies, the Manufaƈtures of their own Country; Mafters of all the Inftances of Infraƈtion of former Treaties, which occafioned the War we are now engaged in: In a Word, Men whofe Rank and Confequence amongft ourfelves, may command Refpeƈt, and procure them Authority, amongft our Enemies; and who to every other Qualification, already enumerated, can boaft of an Integrity not to be corrupted, and a Steadinefs in fupporting the Interefts of their Country, which no Difficulties can difcourage, and no Temptations can fhake: —— Such are the Men, whom you muft endeavour to employ, in the approaching Negociation, and fuch, I hope, ye will be able to find; though, I own, I am puzzled to guefs on whom the Choice will fall, none being, as yet, pointed out by the public Voice, nor, perhaps, fixed upon, by yourfelves. Times have been, when we might have expeƈted,

to

fee *One* named to fuch an important Office, meer-
ly becaufe he was a Favourite, or a Favourite's Favourite ; becaufe he was connected with this Minifter, or was a Relation of that great Man. But if
we have too frequently trified with our national
Concerns, by trufting them in fuch Hands, I need
not fay that there are Circumftances at prefent
which give us reafonable Ground for hoping that
the fame Sagacity, and Defire to ferve the Public
which hath found out, and employed the propereft
Perfons to conduct the Operations of the War, will
be exerted to find out the propereft Perfons (few
as there are to be found) to conduct the Deliberations of the Treaty.

And very deplorable indeed muft be the Inabilities of the Perfons we fhall employ, if their Negociations for Peace be conducted fo awkwardly as to
rob us of the Advantages we have gained by the
War. If we may judge from late Events, *France*
feems as little to abound with Wifdom in the Cabinet, as it doth with Courage and Conduct in the
Field. And if the Negociations at *Utrecht*, in
which almoft all the Advantages of a War equally
fuccefsful with the prefent, were given up, be urg-
ed as an Inftance of the fuperior Dexterity of *French*
Politics, it ought to be remembered that this was
more owing to our own Divifions, than to *their*
Sagacity, and to the Inabilities of our Plenipotentiaries at *Utrecht*, tho' we had no great Reafon, God
knows, to brag of them. What, therefore, may
we not expect from a Negociation to be begun in
very different Circumftances ; when there exifts no
Faction whofe Intereft it may be to perplex and defeat it ; and when that national Unanimity to which
we, in a great Meafure, owe the Succefs of the
War, will ftill continue to exert it's bleffed Effects,
till it make us happy with a fafe and honourable
Peace ?

Peace?—However, favourable as thefe Circumftances are, the Choice of fuch Plenipotentiaries as may be likely to conduct the Negociation,
with Dignity, Dexterity and Integrity, becomes a
Confideration which the Public will expect fhould
be weighed with the utmoft Attention. And, if
fuch Perfons cannot be found amongft us (which I
hope may not be the Cafe) there is a very defirable
Alternative ftill in your Power. Fix the Scene of
Negociation, where, indeed, for the Honour of
our Country, I could wifh to fee it fixed, name no
other Plenipotentiaries to conduct the Peace but
thofe Minifters who directed the War: And a
Treaty of *London*, in fuch Hands, will make ample
Amends for our wretched Management at *Utrecht*.

But let Peace be never fo well made; let Minifters plan Treaties with the greateft Sagacity, and
Plenipotentiaries negociate the Articles with the utmoft Skill and Dexterity, yet we know from Hiftory and Obfervation, that they never can be perpetual,
and, moft commonly, are not lafting. Princes, too
frequently, feem to own no other Rule of Action,
than prefent Convenience; and the Law of Nations
is feldom appealed to, but to fanctify Injuftice, and
fave Appearances. Nor are the pofitive Compacts
folemnly agreed upon between Nation and Nation,
better obferved. For how feldom do we fee a
Treaty religioufly adhered to, by the Parties whofe
Intereft it is to break it, and who think they are in
fuch Circumftances as to be able to break it with
Impunity?—If fuch Infidelity be too common a-
mongft Princes in general, Experience, long Experience teaches us, that the Nation with whom
we are foon to treat, excel us, at leaft, in this
Part of Policy. For no Cords are ftrong enough
to bind them.

Gallic

Gallic Faith is become proverbial, and the Neighbours of *France* can reproach her with innumerable Inftances of a moft profligate Difregard to the moft folemn Treaties. And the Reafon feems to be obvious, without fuppofing that Nation more perfidious than others. The Power, the Populoufnefs, the Extent, the Strength of the *French* Monarchy, free them from thofe Apprehenfions which bind the weaker Side to be faithful to it's Engagements ; and depending upon the Inability of their Neighbours, confidered fingly, to procure to themfelves Juftice, this, too frequently, has tempted them to the moft fhameful and barefaced Inftances of national Breach of Faith.

It well becomes us, therefore, at this Juncture, when the Diftreffes of *France* will oblige them to confent to Terms of Peace, unfavourable to the Intereft, and difgraceful to the Glory of their Monarch, to take every Method in our Power to fecure the Obfervance of thofe Conceffions they may make ; and to infift upon their giving us fuch Proofs of their Sincerity, before any Negociation be entered upon, as may give us fome Affurance that they mean to be more faithful to their future Engagements.

What Proof of their Sincerity, I would recommend it to you to demand, what Conceffions it will be neceffary to infift upon, I fhall beg Leave to mention ; after having firft fatisfied you by a Detail of fome Particulars, that fuch Demands as I would propofe cannot be looked upon as the Infolence of a Conqueror, but as the wife Forefight of a People whom dear bought Expence hath taught the proper Way of doing itfelf Juftice.

It may not, therefore, be unneceffary to place before your Eyes, fome of the moft remarkable Inftances of *French* Perfidy, which have given Rife

C

to all the Troubles of *Europe* for above thefe hundred Years.

The Peace of *Weftphalia* *, while it fecured the
Liberties and Religion of *Germany*, alfo laid the
Foundation of that Power which hath made *France*,
ever fince, the Terror of *Europe*. By this Treaty ª,
the Upper and the Lower *Alface*, a Country of
great Extent, and of infinite Confequence in Point
of Situation, was ceded to *France*. In this Country
there were Ten *Imperial Cities*, whofe Privileges
and Liberties were in the moft folemn Manner fecured by the fame Treaty, which exprefly fays,
ᵇ *that they fhall preferve their Freedom, and that the
King of* France *fhall not affume over them, any Thing
more than the bare Right of Protection.* How was
this Article obferved? The ten Imperial Cities
were foon humbled to receive the *French* Yoke, e-
qually with the reft of *Alface*, and remain, now,
lafting Monuments, what others may expect from
Power unreftrained by Juftice.

The Treaty † of the *Pyrenees* ftill enlarged the
Boundaries of *France*, efpecially on the Side of *Flanders* ; and the *Spaniards* thought themfelves fafe
from farther Loffes, by the Marriage of their In-
fanta to *Louis* the XIV. who, upon that Occafion,
jointly with her, made a formal Renunciation of
all her Rights, to fucceed to any Part of the *Spanifh*
Poffeffions. And yet, with unparalleled Infolence,
feven Years had fcarcely elapfed before *Flanders* was
again attacked, on Pretence of thofe very Rights
which had been fo lately renounced, and which,
even tho' they had not been renounced, muft have

---

* 1648.   ª Article 73, & feq.   ᵇ Article 88.
Le Roi de France ne f'arrogera, fur les villes de la Prefecture,
que le fimple Droit de Protection, qui appartenoit a la Maifon
d' Autriche.   † 1659.

appeared

appeared chimerical, unlefs a Sifter can have a Right to fucceed in Preference to her Brother.

The Peace of *Nimeguen* ‡ reftored the Tranquilquillity of *Europe*, which the Invafion of *Holland* by the *French* had difturbed. But fcarcely was the Peace figned before it was fhametully violared. The Decrees of the Chambers of Re-union, by which *Lewis* the XIV. feized fo many Territories, to which he has not the leaft Right ; the Surprifal of *Strafburgh*, and the Blockade of *Luxemburgh*, fhewed fuch a Wantonnefs of Perfidy, as no Hiftory of the moft barbarous and unpolifhed Savages could well exceed ; and juftly drew upon the common Oppreffor, the joint Vengeance of offended *Europe*.

Who is ignorant of the Story of the *Partition* Treaty ? Solemnly ratified and agreed to preferve that Tranquillity which the Treaty of *Refwyck* had juft reftored to *Europe*, it was no fooner made than it was fhamefully abandoned by the Court of *France* ; and for fuch Reafons as will, upon every Occafion, juftify every Injuftice. The *Letter* of the Treaty, indeed, was violated, they muft own ; —but the *Spirit* of it was what ought to be attended to. And by fuch a Comment, worthier of a pitiful Sophifter, than of a moft Chriftian King, his Grandfon was affifted in placing himfelf on the Throne of *Spain*.

The Politics of *Lewis* the XV. have been faithfully copied from thofe of his Great-Grandfather ; and the Behaviour of *France*, upon the Death of *Charles* the VI. is a frefh Proof, of how little Ufe are the moft folemn Treaties, with a Power that knows no Ties but thofe of Intereft. —The Treaty of *Vienna* had but two or three Years before *, an-

‡ 1679.   * In 1738.

nexed

nexed to the Crown of *France*, the Dutchy of *Lorrain*; a Ceſſion which was purchaſed, and purchaſed cheaply, by the Guarantee of the † *Pragmatic Sanction*. By this Stipulation, *France* was under the moſt ſolemn Engagements to ſupport the Queen of *Hungary* in the Poſſeſſion of all her Father's Dominions. But how was the Engagement fulfilled? Poſterity will ſcarcely believe ſuch bare-faced Perfidy was poſſible, as our Times ſaw was actually avowed upon that Occaſion. *Germany* was, inſtantly, covered with the Armies of *France*, to aſſiſt the Elector of *Bavaria*, in an Attempt to overturn the *Pragmatic Sanction* ſo lately guaranteed by them, and to dethrone that Princeſs whom they were bound by a Treaty, ſworn to in the Name of the Holy Trinity, to protect and defend from all her Enemies.

I have brought down this Sketch of *French* Faith to the preſent Times; imperfect indeed; but, as far as it goes, ſtrictly conformable to Hiſtorical Truth.——What Confidence then, can *France* expect any of it's Neighbours will put in her, after ſo many and ſuch flagrant Inſtances of national Perjury, as ſhe appears to be guilty of?——The Catalogue of her Infidelities will ſtill be encreaſed; and the little Reaſon that our Iſland, in particular, has to truſt Her, will ſtill be more apparent, by reminding you of ſome of the many Proofs, which *Great Britain* itſelf can appeal to, of *French* Ingenuity in Treaty-breaking.—I ſhall go no higher than the Peace of *Utrecht*, becauſe the Inſtances in which it hath been violated by *France*, have produced the preſent War; and becauſe the Enumeration of them will lead me, naturally, to thoſe Hints which I mean to throw out, as neceſſary to be at-

† Treaty of Vienna, Article 10:

tended

tended to in our future Negociations; and which, if neglected, will lofe to this Nation all the Fruits of thofe Succefles, to gain which, we have ftrained every Nerve, and loaded ourfelves with a Burthen under which it is a Miracle that we have not already funk.

The War which was clofed by the Peace of *Utrecht* had been undertaken with Views confined, altogether, to the Continent of *Europe*, and carried on, though at an immenfe Expence, more to gain Conquefts for our Allies than for ourfelves. However, in the Treaty of Peace, fome Advantages and Conceffions were ftipulated in Favour of the Crown of *Great Britain*, and it's commercial Interefts.

By the 12th Article[a], All *Nova Scotia or Acadia, with it's ancient Limits, and with all it's Dependencies, is ceded to the Crown of Great Britain.*

And by the 15th Article, *The Subjects of France, Inhabitants of Canada, and elfewhere, fhall not difturb or moleft, in any Manner whatever, the Five Indian Nations which are fubject to Great Britain, nor it's other American Allies.*

Let us now fee how thefe Articles have been obferved. The *French* feem to have had two *Capital Views* in all their *American* Schemes, ever fince they have thought Trade and Commerce an Object worthy of their Attention. The firft was to extend themfelves from *Canada*, Southwards, through the Lakes, along the Back of our Colonies; by which Means they might anfwer a double Purpofe, of cutting off our Communication with the *Indian Nations*, and of opening a Communication for themfelves, between the Rivers *St. Lawrence* and *Mifsifippi*, and thus to join, as it were, their Colo-

---

[a] Not having, in my Poffeffion, an Original Copy of the Treaty of Utrecht, I have made Ufe of *Lamberti*'s Tranflation.

nies of *Canada* and *Louisiana*. The other Part of
their Plan, equally important, and more immediately fatal to our Interests in *North America*, was
to gain a Communication with the Ocean; the only
Access they now have to *Canada*, through the River *St. Lawrence*, being shut up half the Year.

Full of this favorite Project of *American* Empire, soon after the Treaty of *Utrecht*, they began
to enlarge their Boundaries on that Continent, in
direct Violation of the solemn Concessions they had
so lately made.

As long ago as 1720, they seized and fortified
the most important Pass in *America*, at *Niagara*;
in that very Country of the five *Indian Nations*,
from which the 15th Article of the Treaty of *U-
trecht* had excluded them. The infinite Consequence of *Niagara* made them less scrupulous, no
Doubt, about Treaties. For by Means of this U-
surpation they, in a Manner, became Masters of
the Lakes, and could, at Leisure, extend themselves to the *Ohio*, and carry their Chain of Forts
and Settlements down to the *Mississippi*.

The Plan of Usurpation on the Back of our Colonies went on gradually and successfully from
Year to Year; the *Indians* owned by the Peace of
Utrecht to be our Subjects, were debauched from
our Interest, and spirited up to massacre, and scalp
the *English*; and in 1731, the Insolence of the
French grew to such an Height, that they erected
their Fort at *Crown-Point*, in a Country indisput-
ably ours; whether considered as in the Center of
the *five Nations*, or as actually within the Limits of
New-York. And whoever casts his Eye upon the
Situation of this Fort, in the Map, will see how
greatly the Possession of it facilitated the Comple-
tion of the great Object of opening a Communication with the Ocean; and, how much it exposed

our

our moſt valuable Colonies to *Indian* Maſſacres and *French* Invaſions.

If it ſhould be aſked, what was our Miniſtry in *England* employed about, during ſuch Inſtances of *French* Perfidy—the Anſwer muſt be, (tho' I wiſh I could draw a Veil over this Period) that our Affairs were then conducted by a Miniſter who was awake, indeed, to every Scheme of Corruption; eager to buy a Borough, or to bribe a Member; but ſlow to every Meaſure of national Importance and Utility. His firſt, his only Object, was to preſerve himſelf in Power; and as, in Proſecution of ſuch intereſted and mercenary Views, he had actually engaged this Nation in an Alliance with *France*, in *Europe*, (to pull down the exorbitant Power of our old and natural Ally) it was no Wonder, that he heard unmoved, and ſuffered with Impunity, the *French* Uſurpations in *North America*.

Let us next trace the *French* Infidelity with Regard to *Nova Scotia* or *Acadia*. Tho' that Province had been yielded to us at *Utrecht*, we had taken very few Steps to ſettle it effectually, till 1749, after the Peace of *Aix la Chapelle*. And then the *French* Court gave us a Specimen of *Chicane* worthy, indeed, of thoſe whom no Treaty ever bound, in Oppoſition to their Convenience: They began to ſpeak out, and to tell us, nay to inſiſt upon it ſeriouſly in Memorials, that the Country ceded to us under the Name of *Nova Scotia*, comprehended only the *Peninſula*, and did not extend beyond the *Iſthmus*. Whereas the Charters of King *James* I. to Sir *William Alexander*; and Sir *William*'s own Map as old as the Charter, demonſtrate that the *ancient Limits* of the Country ſo named included a vaſt Tract of Land, beſides the *Peninſula*, reaching along the Coaſt till it joined *New England*; and extending up the

3   Country

Country till it was bounded by the South Side of the River St. *Laurence.* Of fuch an Extent of Country they had formed a Plan to rob us; hoping, no Doubt, to find the fame Supinenefs in the *Britifh* Adminiftration which had overlooked their former Encroachments. With this View they defired that Commiffaries might meet to fettle the Limits, promifing not to act in *America*, till thofe Commiffaries fhould agree, or the Conferences break up. But how was this Promife obferved ? While the Commiffaries trifled away their Time at *Paris*, the Ufurpations went on in *America* ; Incurfions were frequently made into the Peninfula of *Acadia*, the Poffeffion of which they did not pretend to difpute with us; Forts were built by them in feveral Places, and particularly a moft important One to command the *Ifthmus* ; thus deciding by the Sword, in Time of full Peace, that Controverfy which they themfelves had agreed fhould be amicably adjufted by their Commiffaries; and furnifhing a lafting Warning to us, that a Treaty which leaves Points of Confequence to be determined by any after Conferences, only ferves to light up another War.

While the *French* Ufurpations went on fo infolently in *Nova Scotia* ; the Plan was carrying on with equal Perfidy on the Banks of the *Ohio* ; a Country, the Inhabitants of which had been in Alliance with the *Englifh* above an hundred Years ago ; an Alliance frequently renewed ; to which alfo we had a Claim as being a Conqueft of the *Five Nations*, and from which, therefore, the *French* were excluded by the 15th Article of the Treaty of *Utrecht* above recited. But what avail Treaties when Intereft comes in Competition ? The Poffeffion of the *Ohio* was abfolutely neceffary, that the great Plan of connecting *Canada* with
Louifi-

Louisiana might succeed: And, therefore, they began their Hostilities against us, in that Country, the very Year of the Peace of *Aix-la Chapelle*; opposed our Plan of a New Settlement (which had been thought of by us above forty Years before) insulted our Traders, plundered and made them Prisoners; and in 1754 having defeated *Washington*, and destroyed *our* Fort, they built *their Fort Du Quesne*; and Troops were sent daily from *France* to secure the Possession of this, and of their new and important Usurpations.

No Doubt the *French* Ministers flattered themselves that *England*, inattentive to the Interests of its Colonies for so many Years before, and who, so lately, had submitted to a Disadvantageous Peace, would not have the Spirit to oppose Force to Force, and do itself Justice by other Weapons than the Complaints of Lord *Albemarle*, and the Memorials of Mr. *Mildmay*. But the Hour of Vengeance was, at last, come; the Interests of the Kingdom were attended to by those in Power; the infinite Importance of our *American* Colonies was understood, and a Resolution taken to have Recourse to Arms. And thus *England*, which, for half a Century, had been engaged in every Body's Quarrels but its own; wasting its Millions, and lavishing its Blood, to obtain a Barrier in *Flanders*, which those for whom we conquered it could not defend, or rather did not think it worth while to keep; began the present War, a War truly *NATIONAL.*

If there be Merit in this spirited Conduct, tell your Enemies, *My Lord*, that you, and a near Relation of yours (whose Memory always will be respected) had then the chief Direction of public Business. And you, *Sir*, will pardon me for paying this Compliment to those who began the War

D   *with*

with Spirit; while I, at the fame Time, declare it as my Opinion that your coming into Power after it was begun, has contributed to its being carried on with a Succefs equally glorious and important to the Nation.

But before I make the Application of the above Deduction concerning * our *American* Complaints (which I fhall, by and bye, make Ufe of, when I come to fpeak to the Terms which it will be *neceffary* to infift upon at the approaching Treaty) it will be proper to mention another moft important Inftance of *French* Perfidy in *Europe*.

Dunkirk, by its Situation almoft oppofite the Mouth of the *Thames*, had done amazing Mifchief to the Trade of *England*, during King *William's* and Queen *Anne's* Wars. The Demolition of *Dunkirk*, therefore, very naturally become a favourite Object of the Nation; the Parliament, in 1708, addreffed her Majefty to make no Peace without this Condition †; and tho' after a War fo fuccefsful, much more might have been obtained for *England* than really

* For the Particulars of the *French* Encroachments in *America*, which I have only given a Sketch of, fee the Memorials of our Commiffaries, Dr. *Mitchell's* Conteft in *America*; the Doctor's and Mr. *Evan's* Maps, and many other Treatifes.

† *March* 2d 1708. The Lords having fent down an Addrefs to the Commons for their Concurrence, relating to certain Conditions to be infifted upon, as the *fine qua non*, of a Treaty with *France*, Mr. Secretary *Boyle* reprefented, That the *Britifh* Nation having been at a vaft Expence of Blood and Treafure, for the Profecution of this neceffary War, it was but juft they fhould reap fome Benefit by the Peace: And the Town of *Dunkirk* being a Neft of Pyrates, that infefted the Ocean and did infinite Mifchief to Trade, He, therefore, moved that the demolifhing of its Fortifications and Harbours be infifted upon, in the enfuing Treaty of Peace, and inferted in the Addrefs, which wa unanimoufly approved of, and carried back to the Lords. See *Chandler's* Debates of Parliament, Vol. vii. p. 122.

was,

was, this Point was carefully infifted upon, and the Ninth Article of the Peace of *Utrecht* obtained.

By this Article, *The* French *King engages to demolifh all the Fortifications of the City of* Dunkirk ; *to ruin the Harbour : to break the Dykes and Sluices— The Works towards. the Sea to be deftroyed in Two Months, and thofe to the Land in Three Months after ; all this to be done at his own Expence ; and the Fortifications, Harbour, Dykes and Sluices, never after to be reftored.* Could Words be devifed in all the Extent of Language to ftipulate, in a ftronger Manner, the effectual and fpeedy Demólition of this Place? And yet all *Europe* faw with Amazement, and *England* beheld with Indignation, the Peace of *Utrecht* violated, with Regard to this important Condition, almoft as foon as it was figned.

By the Article above-recited we fee that *Dunkirk* was to be demolifhed within five Months after the figning the Peace ; and yet, near an Year after, I find Mr. *Walpole*, in our Houfe of Commons, infifting that the Peace had already been broken with Regard to *Dunkirk* ; *Since inftead of ruining the Harbour, the* French *were then actually repairing the Sluices, and working on a new Canal* *. And tho' the pacific Inclinations of the Miniftry in 1713, when Mr. *Walpole* pufhed this Affair, over-ruled the Inquiry, the Facts on which it would have proceeded were certain.

The *fpirited* Remonftrances of Lord *Stair* at *Paris*, on the Acceffion of *George* I. concerning this Infraction of the Peace, were the laft Inftances of Humiliation which *Lewis* XIV. faw himfelf expofed to ; and, perhaps, he would have found himfelf obliged to do us that Juftice, by Necef-

---

* Chandler's Debates, Vol. 8. p. 69.

fity,

fity, which the *Regent*, who foon after came into
Power, willingly agreed to from Views of *private
Intereſt*. Tho' the Peace of *Utrecht* had obliged
the *Spaniſh* Branch of the *Bourbon* Family to renounce their Right of Succeſſion to the Crown of
France, the Duke of *Orleans*, who, by this Regulation, faw only an Infant's Life between him and
the Throne, knew well, that tho' the Renunciation
had been folemnly fworn to, the Doctrine of its
Invalidity, of its being an Act, void, *ab initio*,
had been publickly avowed. *Torcy*, as appears
by his * Correfpondence with Lord *Bolingbroke*,
very frankly made no Scruple of telling the *Eng-
liſh* before Hand, that this Expedient, which had
been devifed to prevent the Union of *France* and
Spain under one Monarch, would be of little Force,
as being inconfiftent with the fundamental Laws
of *France*; by this Declaration giving us a very
remarkable Inftance of the Weaknefs or of the
Wickednefs of our then Minifters, who could
build the Peace of *Europe* on fo fandy a Foundation, and accept of Terms which *France* itfelf was
honeft enough to own were not to be kept.

However, the *Regent* was refolved to fupport
his Claim to the Crown of *France*, in Exclufion

* See the Report of the fecret Committee, p. 13. The fol-
lowing Extract from a Letter of Monfr. *Torcy* to Mr. *St. John*
is remarkable. " The Renunciation defired would be null and
" invalid by the fundamental Laws of *France*; according to
" which Laws the moft near Prince to the Crown is, of Ne-
" ceffity, the Heir thereto.—This Law is looked upon, as the
" Work of him who hath eftablifhed all Monarchies, and we
" are perfuaded in *France* that God only can abolifh it. No
" Renunciation, therefore, can deftroy it; and if the King of
" *Spain* fhould renounce it for the Sake of Peace, and in Obe-
" dience to the King his Grandfather, they would deceive them-
" felves that received it as a fufficient Expedient to prevent the
" Mifchief we propofe to avoid."

to the *Spanish* Branch ; and as the Support and Affiftance of *England* was neceffary for this Purpofe, it is not to be wondered at that he fhould court the Friendfhip of a Nation from whom he had fo much to expect; and, therefore, he was wife enough to do us Juftice, by carrying into Execution, in fome Degree, the Article relating to *Dunkirk*.

The perfonal Intereft of the Regent was the only Reafon for this Compliance : But fucceeding Adminiftrations in *France* not being influenced by the fame private Views to adhere to Treaties folemnly ratified, *Dunkirk* began gradually to rife from its Ruins ; its Port again received Ships ; its Trade flourifhed ; *England* faw itfelf deprived of this favourite Advantage gained at *Utrecht* ; and fuch was the Afcendancy of *French* Councils over thofe of this Ifland, at the Period I fpeak of, that we were actually engaged in Alliances with *France*, while that Nation was thus openly infulting us, and infulting us, without Obftruction, in fo effential an Article. We all remember what paffed in Parliament in 1733, relating to the Point now before us.——Such was the tame Acquiefcence of the *British* Adminiftration, that *Dunkirk*, by this Time, ftood upon our Cuftom-Houfe Books as a Port, from whence great Imports were made ; and when an Inquiry concerning this was propofed in the Houfe of Commons by a great Parliament Man *, fince dead, the then Minifter hung his Head, in the Houfe, for Shame. And who could have believed it poffible, that the fame Perfon, who had been fo ready to promote a Parliamentary Inquiry into this Violation of the Peace in 1713, fhould obftruct fuch an Inquiry, when he

* Sir William Wyndham.

him-

himfelf was in Power, tho' the Reafons for it had become much ftronger ? Who could fee Him, without Indignation, fhut his Eyes to the Re-eftablifhment of *Dunkirk*, and obftruct the propofed Inquiry, by getting from Cardinal *Fleury* (who then governed *France*, and, I blufh to fay it, *England* too) a delufive, minifterial Letter, promifing what he knew would not be performed ;—and obtained, perhaps, only becaufe the Cardinal was affured, that the Breach of the Promife would not be refented ?

While *England* remained fo averfe to do itfelf Juftice, no Wonder that *France* improved the Opportunity. At the Time when that *Minifter* was obliged to retire from Power, the Re-eftablifhment of *Dunkirk* was completed. For, within a few Months after *, we find a Memorial prefented by Lord *Stair* to the *Dutch*, complaining of this Violation of the Peace of *Utrecht*, and urging this as a Reafon for their joining us againft *France*. And as it is for the Honour of the Adminiftration then entering into Office, that they began with Meafures fo fpirited and national, it is equally remarkable, that the fame Perfon, who had threatened *Louis* XIV. in his own Palace, for his Slownefs in demolifhing *Dunkirk*, lived to be again employed by his Country at the Diftance of near thirty Years, when the Reftoration of *Dunkirk* became an Object of national Refentment.

The two Nations had not, as yet, begun the late War, when we faw, in *One* Inftance, both a Proof that *Dunkirk* was again a *Port*, and a Port which may be made Ufe of, to endanger the Safety of *Britain*. At the Time I now fpeak of †, we

* The Memorial is dated *July* 1, 1742.

† In 1743-4.

be=

beheld the Harbour of *Dunkirk* crowded with Tranfports to embark Count *Saxe* and the *Pretender* to invade us. And, if that Invafion had then taken Effect, from that very *Port* which was to be no *Port* (happily the Winds were contrary to the Fleet from *Breft*) the infinite Mifchief which this Nation may fuffer from its Re-eftablifhment, would have been fatally experienced.

Though we have no great Reafon to brag of the Treaty made at the Conclufion of the laft War (which I am afhamed to call a Peace, as it fettled nothing that was before in Doubt between the two Nations) the Peace of *Utrecht* concerning *Dunkirk*, was, neverthelefs in its moft effential Part, reftored to its full Force. I fay, in its moft *Effential Part*; becaufe, though the 17th Article of the Treaty of *Aix-la-Chapelle* left *Dunkirk* in the State it then was, with Regard to its Fortifications to the Land ; the fame Article revived our Right, to the Demolition of its Port, by ftipulating *That ancient Treaties are to be obferved in Regard to the Port, and the Works on the Sea fide.*

Little or nothing was done between the Conclufion of the Peace, and the breaking out of the prefent War, towards carrying into Execution this frefh Promife. On the contrary, the enlarging of the Fortifications of *Dunkirk*, is mentioned in his Majefty's Declaration of War, three Years ago, as one of the frefh Heads of Injury offered to *England.* And whoever reflects upon the Tranfactions, fince that Period, will fee that *Dunkirk* is reftored to its original Importance. Its Privateers have done infinite Mifchief to our Trade ; a Squadron of his Majefty's Navy, in vain blocked up its Harbour lately, to prevent the failing of *Thurot*'s Fleet ; and, it is well known, that the long threatened Invafion of thefe Kingdoms, which *France*, in Defpair, certainly meditated, would
have

have been attempted from this Place, if the Deſtruction of their Ships of War by *Hawke*, had not taught them the Abſurdity of invading us in their much celebrated *flat bottom Boats*, which, we may well ſuppoſe, will hardly be tried, when their Fleets, really formidable, have been deſtroyed in the Attempt.

The above Enumeration of *French* Infidelities, in general, and in particular their Behaviour to *England* with regard to *Dunkirk*, and with regard to *North-America*, ſo naturally points out the *Expediency*, and *Neceſſity* of the Hints I ſhall now offer, that, in propoſing them, I may well hope not to have them ridiculed as the Reveries of a chimerical *St. Pierre*, but rather attended to, as the ſober Dictates of Prudence, and of a Zeal not altogether devoid of Knowlege.

Firſt, Then, *my Lord and Sir*, before you enter upon any New Treaty, or liſten to any plauſible Propoſals whatever, inſiſt that Juſtice may be done this Nation, with regard to former Treaties. Shew *France* the ſtrong, the ſolemn Engagement ſhe entered into at *Utretcht* to demoliſh *Dunkirk*; put her in Mind of the amazing Perfidy with which ſhe, from Time to Time, eluded the Performance of that Engagement; and demand *immediate* Juſtice on that Article, as a preliminary Proof of her Sincerity in the enſuing Negociation.

Be not deceived any longer in this Matter. The *French* will, no doubt, aſſure you that the Demolition of *Dunkirk* ſhall be an Article in the New Treaty. But let them know, you are not to be *ſo* impoſed upon. They will, to be ſure, when this becomes a new Article, reckon it a new Conceſſion on their Side, and expect ſomething in return for it,—perhaps *Guadaloupe*, or ſome ſuch Trifle, as they will call it. But tell them with the Firmneſs of wiſe Conquerors, that the Demolition of
Dunkirk

Dunkirk is what you are intitled to by Treaties made long ago, and violated ; and that it fhall not be fo much as mentioned in the infuing Negociation, but complied with, before that Negociation fhall commence.

Or, admitting that no Conceffion fhould be required by *France* in the New Treaty, in Confideration of a New Article to demolifh *Dunkirk*, place to them, in the ftrongeft Light, the unanfwerable Reafons we have againft putting any Confidence in them, that fuch an Article would be better executed, than that in the treaty of *Utrecht* has been.

If they refufe doing us this immediate Juftice, previous to the Peace ; afk them how they can expect that we fhould have any Reliance on their Sincerity to fulfill the New Engagements they may enter into, when they afford us fo ftrong, fo glaring an Inftance of Infidelity, in an Article of fuch Confequence, made fo many Years ago ? Can you have any Dealings with a Power, who, if he refufes this, at the very Time he is treating, affords you fuch manifeft Proof, that his Word is not to be relied upon, and that you cannot truft to the Execution of any Promife ever fo folemnly made ?

Perhaps *France* may think it a Difgrace to them, to comply with any Thing previous to the beginning of a Negociation. Tell them, that acting honourably, and doing what Juftice requires, can never be difgraceful. But if it be a Difgrace, tell them, with the Spirit of honeft Men, that we owe it them, for the greater Difgrace they put, not long ago, upon us, by requiring us to fend two Peers of this Realm to remain in *France* as *Hoftages*, till we furrendered *Louifburg* ; an Indignity which I cannot call to mind, without Pain ; and which, I always thought was fubmitted to without Neceffity.

E   It

It is now our Turn to vindicate the Honour of our Nation ; and as *Dunkirk* was put into our Poffeffion before the Treaty of *Utrecht*, as a Pledge of the *French* Sincerity, and to continue in our Poffeffion, till the Demolition fhould be completed ; let fome fuch Expedient be now agreed upon ; with this Difference only, that inftead of *five Months after the Peace*, the Time fixed, for the Demolition, at *Utrecht*, let no Peace be figned, at prefent, till this Right acquired to us by former Treaties, and of which we have been fo perfidioufly robbed, be actually carried into full Execution.

However, if any infuperable Difficulties fhould attend the doing ourfelves Juftice, on this Head, before the Peace ; if, for Inftance, which perhaps may be the Cafe, it fhould be found that it cannot be complied with, un'efs we confent to a *Ceffation of Arms*, during the Time of Negociation ; rather than give *France* that Opportunity of recovering from its Diftreffes, and of being protected from the Superiority of our Arms, before we have, finally, obliged them to accept of our own Terms of Peace (which was one Caufe of the Ruin of our Negociation at *Utrecht*) I would wave infifting upon the Demolition of *Dunkirk*, before the Treaty, and think it fufficient to demand *Hoftages* from them, as a Security that it fhall be faithfully complied with, within a limited Time after the Treaty fhall be concluded. The *Parifians* had two *Englifh Milords* to ftare at, upon the laft Peace ; and I do not fee why the Curiofity of our *Londoners* fhould not be gratified, in the fame Way ; and Two *Ducs & Pairs* of *France* be fent as Hoftages to *England*, till *Dunkirk* ceafe to be a Port.

I know well, that Political Opinions, concerning the Importance of any particular Object, are as frequently dictated by Whim and Fafhion, as built

on

on folid Reafon and Experience. Perhaps, fome
may think, that this is the Cafe, with Regard to
the Neceffity of demolifhing *Dunkirk*. But, tho'
it may not at prefent be fo favorite an Object of
National Politics, as it was in the Queen's Time ;
this has not been owing to any real Change of Circumftances ; but to another Caufe, to the *American*
Difputes between the two Nations, which have
been the great Object of the prefent War, and
fcarcely permitted us, hitherto, to reflect, in what
other Inftances, the Infidelities of *France* muft be
checked at the infuing Peace.——But as this defirable Event now approaches, we cannot forget, or
forgive the Behaviour of our Enemies with Regard
to *Dunkirk* ; and it will be equally neceffary for the
Honour and for the *Intereft* of this Nation to make
no Peace, without obtaining full Satisfaction on
this Head. It will be neceffary for the *Honour* of
the Nation to infift upon this, if it were only, to
fhew to *Europe* in general, and to *France* in particular—That we have too much Spirit not to refent
Injuries ; and too much Wifdom not to take Care,
when we have it happily in our Power, to prevent
them for the future.—But the Demolition of *Dunkirk*, is alfo neceffary, if we would take Care of
the Intereft of the Nation. Such hath been our
Succefs, in deftroying the Navy of *France* ; and fo
unable doth that Kingdom now appear, to carry on
its ambitious Projects by Land, and to vie at the
fame Time, with *England*, for Dominion on the
Sea ; that we may reafonably fuppofe, there is an
End of *Breft* and *Toulon* Squadrons, to face our
Fleets ; and a future War with *England*, will leave
the *French* no other Way of diftreffing us by Sea,
than to lie in watch for our Merchant Ships, with
numberlefs Privateers. In fuch a piratical War,
Dunkirk, if its Harbour be not now deftroyed,

E 2 will,

will, too late, be found to be of infinite Confequence ; and we fhall fatally experience it again,
what it was in the Queen's Time, and in the Language of her Parliament, *a Neft of Pyrates, in-
fefting the Ocean, and doing infinite Mifchief to
Trade* *.

For thefe Reafons, therefore, I am fo *old-fafhion-
ed* as to expect that our Plenipotentiaries will have
this Point properly ftated to them in their Inftruc-
tions, and that *Delenda eft Carthago, Demolifh Dunkirk,* will be a Preliminary Article in the enfuing
Negociation.

The War having begun, principally, with a
View to do ourfelves Juftice in *North America,* the
Regulation of Matters, on that Continent, ought
to be, and no Doubt, will be, the capital Article
relating to *England,* in the coming Treaty. It
will be neceffary, therefore, to give you my Sentiments, on this Head ; and while I do it, with all
becoming Diffidence, I fhall, at the fame Time,
fupport what I may offer, with Reafons appearing
fo ftrong to me, as may perhaps recommend it to
your farther Confideration, though it fhould fail of
producing Conviction.

Now it is with the greateft Pleafure, I would
obferve, that with Regard to *North America,* we
have nothing to afk, at the Peace, which we have
not already made ourfelves Mafters of, during the
War We have been bleffed by Heaven, with a
Succefs, in that Part of the World, fcarcely to be
paralleled in Hiftory. The Rafhnefs of *Braddock,*
the Inexperience of *Shirley,* the Inactivity of *Lou-
doun,* and the Ill-fuccefs of *Abercrombie,* feem only
to have been fo many neceffary Means of producing
that Unanimity in our Colonies, that Spirit in our

* See above, p. 18.

Troops ;

Troops ; and that steady Perseverance in our Ministers, as hath not only recovered from the Enemy
all his Usurpations, but *Louisburg* is an *English*
Harbour ; *Quebec*, the Capital of *Canada*, is already in our Possession ; and the Rest of that
Country will fall of Course. It is a Prospect still
more agreeable ; that by destroying the Naval
Force of *France*, our *North American* Conquests
cannot be retaken ; and the Principle I would now
lay down, and which I would recommend it to you
to adopt, *is, not to give up any of them*. And I
shall now endeavour to prove to you, that such a
Demand may be insisted upon, without giving the
Enemy any Pretence for accusing us of Insolence towards them ; and cannot be omitted without giving the Nation just Reason to complain, that we
have consented to a *treacherous* and *delusive*
Peace.

It cannot, surely, ever enter the Imagination of a
British Administration, to make Peace, without,
at least, keeping in our Possession, all those Places,
where the *French* had settled themselves, in Violation of former Treaties, and from which we have,
fortunately, driven them. Upon this Plan, then,
we shall, at the Peace, be left in Possession not only
of the *Peninsula* of *Acadia*, but of All *Nova Scotia*,
according to its old Limits ; the Bay of *Fundi*, and
the River *St. John*.—The important Conquests of
Crown Point, and *Niagara*, will not be relinquish-
ed ; and *Fort du Quesne*, and the Country near the
Ohio, will remain Ours.——They are already Ours ;
the *French* know they cannot get them back during
the War, and they do not expect that we shall give
them up at the *Peace*.

But though Care should be taken to keep all
those Places just mentioned ; something more must
be done, or our *American* Colonies will tell you you
have

have done *Nothing*. In a Word, you muſt keep *Canada*, otherways you lay the Foundation of an--other War.

The Neceſſity of this may be placed in ſo ſtrik-ing a View, as to ſilence the *French* Plenipotentia-ries, and to convince all *Europe*, of the *Juſtice* of our Demand.

Aſk the *French*, what Security they can give you, if we reſtore *Canada* to them, however re-ſtrained in its Boundaries, that they will not again begin to extend them at our Expence? If the Treaty of *Utrecht* could not keep them from En-croachments, what Reaſon can we have to ſuppoſe the future Treaty will be better obſerved? If the *French* are left at *Montreal*, and the *three Rive s*, can we be certain they will not again croſs the *Champlain Lake*, and attack *Crown-Point*? If the River St. *Lawrence* be ſtill theirs, what is to inſure us againſt an Expedition to *Niagara*? Can we flat-ter ourſelves, that a People, who in full Peace, erected thoſe two ſortreſſes, in direct Violation of their Faith plighted at *Utrecht*, will be reſtrained, by any future Treaty, from attempting, alſo in full Peace, to recover them? After having ſeen the *French* carrying on a regular Plan of Uſurpation, in *North America*, for theſe Forty Years paſt, ſhall we be ſo weak as to believe that they will now lay it aſide? No, depend upon it, if the *French* think it worth their while to aſk back that Part of *North America*, which was their own, they mean to take a proper Opportunity, of *Elbowing all our Colonies round about*, and of reſuming the ſame ambitious Views of Enlargement which the moſt ſacred Ties of former Treaties could not reſtrain.

The Truth of the Matter is, they were tired of *Canada*. The Inclemency of the Climate, the difficult Acceſs to it; and a Trade ſcarcely defray-ing

ing the Expence of the Colony, would long ago
have induced them to abandon it, if the Plan of
extending its Boundaries, at the Expence of the
English; and of opening its Communication with
Louisiana and with the Ocean, had not made them
perievere. —— *Canada* itself is not worth their afk-
ing ; and if they do defire to have it reftored to
them, it can only be with a View to repeat the fame
Injuries and Infidelities, to punifh which, we engaged in the prefent War. Unlefs, therefore, we
be refolved, *with our Eyes open*, to expofe ourfelves to a Repetition of former Encroachments ;
unlefs we would choofe to be obliged to keep great
Bodies of Troops, in *America*, in full Peace, at an
immenfe Expence ; we can never confent to leave
the *French* any Footing in *Canada.* If we do
not exclude them, *abfolutely* and *entirely* from that
Country ; we fhall foon find we have done nothing.
Let the Treaty be drawn ever fo accurately ; let
the Boundaries between *Canada* and our Colonies,
be defcribed ever fo precifely, and regulated ever
fo much, in our Favour ; what has happened already, ought to teach us what we may expect a-
gain; the future Treaty will be obferved no better than the former have been ; Ufurpation and
Encroachment will gradually revive ; and thus fhall
we have thrown away all our Succeffes ; fo many
Millions will have been expended to no Purpofe ;
and the Blood of fo many thoufands of our brave
Countrymen fpilt, only to remind us, that though
we knew how to conquer, we knew not how to improve, perhaps, the only Opportunity we fhall ever
have, of putting it out of the Power of *France* to
violate its Faith.

I take it for granted that, in the future Negociation, the Ifland of *Cape Breton* will follow the
Fate of *Quebec*; I fhall only obferve with Regard

I

to

to it, that though the Harbour and Fortification of *Louisbourg* be of infinite Service to *France*; it can be of little or no Use to *England*, if *Canada* be left to us. It is of Consequence to *France*, as a Retreat to their Ships fishing on the neighbouring Banks of *Newfoundland*; and as a Security to the Entrance of the *Gulph* of *St. Laurence*. But the Possession of *Newfoundland* itself, makes *Louisbourg* of no Utility to the *English*, in the former Respect; and *Halifax*, where we have a good Harbour, answers very nearly the latter Purpose. Upon this View therefore, may we not hope and expect, that, the Necessity of garrisoning *Louisbourg* having ended with the Conquest of *Quebec*, its Fate will be determined, without troubling the *French* Plenipotentiaries? Without waiting for a Congress, let Orders be forthwith sent to demolish it, so as not to leave one Stone upon another, of the Fortifications; to remove the Inhabitants to *Nova Scotia*, a better Country; and to leave the Island, a bare and barren Rock; the State it was in, before the Peace of *Utrecht* gave Leave to *France* to fortify it. If the Right given to the *French* by the 13th Article of the same Peace, to Fish in some Parts of those Seas should be continued (and I could wish to see it continued, as the Refusal of it would be rather unreasonable) let *Cape Breton* unfortified, and ungarrisoned be left open to them; and a few Men of War kept at *Halifax*, will effectually prevent *Louisbourg*'s being again made a Place of Strength.

If you adopt this Measure, I should be inclined to think, *France* will see that you know your true Interests; and that you are resolved steadily to pursue them. And if they should make any Remonstrances against it, tell them they may follow *our* Example and demolish, if they please, the Fortifications of *Mahon*; which we see them possess

with

with as great Indifference as we remember the Circumftances of its Lofs, with Shame: Which, as being of no Ufe to them they will not defire to keep, and which, having been kept, by us, at an Expence, not counterbalanced by its Utility, we fhall not be very fanguine about recovering. Or, rather tell them, that in demolifhing *Louifbourg*, before the Peace, we only copy a former Example given us by themfelves, when their Troops were employed in difmantling the Frontier Towns in *Flanders*, at the very Time that their Plenipotentiaries at *Aix la Chapelle* were confenting to give them up.

The Plan which I have had the Honour of fketching out to you, befides being fo reafonable in itfelf, is perfectly agreeable to that Moderation exprefled by his Majefty, in his Speech, of *not having entered into the War with Views of Ambition.* The Pofleffion of *Canada,* is no View of Ambition; it is the only Security the *French* can give us, for their future Regard to Treaties. We have made other Conquefts, of great Importance, our Management of which will give us fufficient Means of fhewing our Moderation. And though I fhall not prefume to give any Opinion about the future Difpofal of them, I think, however, I may be allowed to hint, that " the Pofleffion of *Guadaloupe,*" an additional fugar ifland, when we have fo many of our own, ought not to be infifted upon fo ftrenuoufly as to make it a neceffary Condition of the Peace. And though " *Senegal* and *Goree*" are of real Importance in the Slave and Gum Trades, our own *African* Settlements have hitherto fupplied us with Slaves, fufficient for our *American* Purpofes: And the Trade for Gum is, perhaps, not of Confequence enough to make us Amends for the annual Mortality, which we already lament, of our brave Countrymen, to guard our *African* Conquefts. The

F   People

People of *England*, therefore, will not, I believe, blame the giving them back, for a valuable Confideration, — provided *Canada* be left to us.

To confider this Affair in its proper Light, it will be neceffary to reflect on the infinite Confequence of *North America* to this Country. Our Colonies there contain above a Million of Inhabitants, who are moftly fupplied with the Manufactures of *Great Britain*; our Trade to them, by employing innumerable Ships, is one great Source of our maritime Strength; by fupporting our Sugar Iflands with their Provifions, and other Neceffaries, they pour in upon us all the Riches of the *Weft Indies*; we carry their Rice, and Tobacco, and Fifh, to all the Markets of *Europe*; they produce Indigo, and Iron; and the whole Navy of *England* may be equipped, with the Products of *Englifh America*. And if, notwithftanding our having loft feveral Branches of Commerce we formerly enjoyed in *Europe* and to the *Levant*, we have ftill more Commerce than ever; a greater Demand for our Manufactures, and a vaft Increafe of our fhipping; what can this be owing to, but to the Trade to our own *American* Colonies; a Trade which the Succeffes of this War, will render, every Day, more and more advantageous? If this Matter, then, be confidered, in the above Light, by thofe whom I now addrefs, they will make our *North American* Conquefts the *fine qua non* of the Peace, as being the only Method of guarding our *invaluable* Poffeffions there, from Ufurpations and Encroachments; and they will look upon every other Conqueft, we have made, *or may make*, in other Parts of the World, as Inftruments put into our Hands by Providence, to enable us to fettle Affairs on the Continent of *Europe*, as advantageoufly to our Allies, as *our* Gratitude could wifh, and as *their* Fidelity doth deferve.

Here,

Here, then, let me change the Scene, and having settled our Affairs in *Canada* (would to God
they were so settled at the Peace!) permit me to fi-
nish my Plan of Negociation, by giving my Sentiments on the Part we ought to act, to obtain a proper Settlement of Affairs in *Germany*.

If a great Number of Allies can make themselves formidable to a common Enemy, during
the Operations of the War, they are apt to ruin
every Advantage they may have gained, by quar-
relling amongst themselves, when they begin their
Negociations for Peace. Like an *Opposition*, in
our Parliament, carried on against an overgrown
Minister, all Sorts of Parties and Connexions, all
Sorts of disagreeing and contradictory Interests,
join against him, at first, as a common Enemy;
and tolerable Unanimity is preserved amongst them,
so long as the Fate of this Parliamentary War con-
tinues in Suspence. But when once they have driven him to the Wall, and think themselves sure
of Victory; the Jealousies and Suspicions, which,
while the Contest depended, had been stifled, break
out; every one who shared in the Fatigue, expects
to share in the Spoils; separate Interests counter-
act each other; separate Negociations are set on
Foot; till at last, by *untimely* and *mercenary* Divisions, they lose the Fruits of their Victory, and
the Object of the common Resentment is able to
make Terms for himself *. —— This was exactly
the Case, in the Contest between *Lewis* XIV. and
the Princes of *Europe* united against him, before
the Peace of *Utrecht*; and the unhappy Divisions of
the Allies (Divisions too likely to have sprung up,

* The true History of the Transaction here alluded to, may,
possibly, some Time or other, appear; though, as yet, we are
persuaded, the World knows very little of it.

even

even tho' there had not been a Party in *England*, who to gratify their private Refentments, blew up the Coals of Diffention) gave the *French* the Means of procuring more favourable Terms of Peace, than they could well have hoped after fo unfuccefsful a War.

I have mentioned this, with a View to obferve, that the Circumftances of the prefent War on the Continent are very different ; no fuch unfortunate Difunion feems poffible to happen to us, though it may happen amongft the Confederates who are engaged on the fame Side with *France*, againft *Hanover* and the King of *Pruffia*.

It may be collected from more than one Hint dropt in the Courfe of this Letter, that I am no Friend to *Continental Meafures* in general ; efpecially fuch continental Meafures as engaged us during the three laft Wars, as Principals ; when we feemed eager to ruin ourfelves, in Support of that *Auftrian* Family whom we now find, with unparalleled Ingratitude, and incredible Folly, in clofe Alliance with *France*.——But the *Continental Meafures* now adopted by *England* were *neceffary*, both with Regard to Our Honour and Our Intereft. *Hanover* has been attacked by *France*, on a Quarrel entirely *Englifh* ; and tho' Care was taken, by the Act of Settlement, that *England* fhould not be involved in Wars on account of *Hanover* ; yet Gratitude, Honour, the Reputation of our Country, every Motive of Generofity, bound us, not to allow the innocent Electorate to be ruined for *England*'s *American* Quarrel with *France*. In Regard to our Intereft, no *Englifh* Minifter, however inflexible, in his Attachment to his native Country, could have devifed the Means of making the beft Ufe of our *American* Conquefts, if the *French* could have treated with *Hanover* in their Hands. It was
with

with a View to prevent this, to oppofe the *French* in their Projects in *Germany*, the Succefs of which would have been fo detrimental to *England*, that we *honeftly* and *wifely* have formed and have maintained the Army *now* commanded by Prince *Ferdinand*; and have entered into an Alliance with the King of *Pruffia*.

But tho' this was a Meafure of Prudence, it was fcarcely poffible for the wifeft Statefmen to forefee all thofe great Confequences which it hath already produced. The Efforts which the *French* have made in *Germany*, and the Refiftance they have there met with by the Care of the *Britifh* Adminiftration; have contributed more than perhaps we could expect, to our Succefs in *America*, and other Parts of the World. Full of the Project of conquering *Hanover*, *France* faw herfelf obliged to engage in exorbitant Expences; Armies were to be paid, and maintained in *Weftphalia* and on the *Rhine*; vaft Sums were to be advanced to the Court of *Vienna* always as indigent as it is haughty; the ravenous *Ruffians*, and the degenerate *Swedes*, would not move, unlefs allured by Subfidies; and the Mouth of every hungry *German* Prince was to be ftopt, with the *Louis D'ors* of *France*. Involved in Expences thus enormous, our Enemies have been prevented from ftrengthening themfelves at Sea, where *England* had moft Reafon to dread their becoming ftrong.

The infinite Advantages which this Nation hath reaped from the *German* War, are indeed now fo well underftood, that we have feen the greateft Enemies of this *Meafure* acknowledge their Miftake.

They now confefs that if we had not refifted *France*, in her Projects of *German* Conquefts, her beft Troops had not been deftroyed; her own Coafts would have been better protected; fhe
would

would have been able to pay more Attention to her *American* Concerns ; *England* might have been threatned, fo ferioufly, with Invafions, as to be afraid of parting with thofe numerous Armies which have conquered, at fuch a D,ftance of Time. In a Word, that univerfal Bankruptcy, which hath crowned the Diftreffes of *France,* and gives *England* greater Reafon of Exultation, than any Event of the War, might have been prevented. It is entirely owing to the *German* Part of the War that *France* appears thus low in the political Scale of Strength and Riches ; that fhe is found to be a finking Monarchy, nay a Monarchy already funk. And, perhaps, it might be an Inquiry worthy of another *Montefquieu,* to affign the *Caufes of the Rife and Fall* of the *French* Monarchy ; and to point out thofe filent Principles of Decay which have, in our Times, made fo rapid a Progrefs, that *France,* in 1712, after upwards of twenty Years almoft conftant War, maintained againft all *Europe,* was ftill more refpectable, and lefs exhaufted than it now appears to be, when the *fingle* Arm of *Great Britain* is lifted up againft her, and the War has lafted no more than three or four Years.

If this then be the State of the War in *Germany* ; if *England* be bound to take a Part in it, by every Motive of Honour and Intereft ; and if the infinite Advantages it hath already produced, be ftated fairly—the Inference I would draw, and which I believe the whole Nation will alfo draw, is, that we fhould continue to exert thofe Endeavours which hitherto have been fo effectual, in defeating the Defigns of *France* to get Poffeffion of *Hanover.*

His Majefty, as Elector of *Hanover,* has no Views of Ambition : His *Country has been attacked only becaufe it belonged to the King* of *Great Britain :* and nothing more is required of us, but to be true to ourfelves, by neglecting no Step that may pre-

ven

vent *Hanover* from falling again into the Hands of *France*, after having been so miraculously rescued from the Contributions of the repacious *Richlieu*, and saved from the *Military Desert* of *Belleisle*.—I need not say any Thing of the Glory acquired by that Army, which notwithstanding it's great Inferiority, hath driven the *French* twice from the *Weser* to the *Rhine*. I shall only observe, that the next Campaign (if another Campaign should preceed the Peace) will, in all Probability, lose us none of the Advantages we have gained, *on that Side*; if our Army, still headed by Prince *Ferdinand* who has already gained so many Laurels, be rendered more formidable, as I hope it will, by sending to it *some Thousands* more of our national Troops; who now, since the Conquest of *Canada*, and the Defeat of the long threatned Invasion, have no other Scene of Action left, but to contribute to another Victory in *Germany*.

It would be a very pleasing Prospect, if we could speak with equal Confidence, and Probability of Success, concerning the future Operations of the King of *Prussia*. However, when we reflect on the amazing Difficulties he has had to struggle with; attacked on every Side by a Number of Confederates, each of whom, singly, one would have thought, an equal Match for his whole Strength; bearing up, at the same Time, against the formidable Power of the House of *Austria*; the brutal Ferocity of the *Russians*; the Attacks of the *Swedes*; the Armies of the Empire; and, at one Time, having the additional Weight of the *French* Arms upon him; when, I say, we reflect on the uncommon Difficulties this magnanimous Prince has to resist, we must rather express our Wonder, and our Satisfaction that his Situation is still so respectable, than indulge our Fears, that it is likely to be worse. The severest eft Checks he has met with during this War, have only ferved to fhew how calm he poffeffes himfelf under Diftrefs, and how ably he can extricate himfelf. The Hour of Adverfity has called forth all his Abilities, and if he has failed fome times, from too great an Eagernefs to conquer, he has always been able to retrieve his Affairs, and like *Anteus*, gained frefh Strength from every Overthrow.

And, upon this Principle, I flatter myfelf, his *Pruffian* Majefty will ftill be able to fecure to himielf the great r Part, if not the whole of *Saxony* for his Winter Quarters, and to recruit his Army, no Doubt much fhattered with it's Loffes and Fatigues, before the opening of another Campaign. It is to be hoped alfo, that befides the amazing Refources He has ftill left in his own unbounded Genius, and the generous and effectual Support which his Connexion with *England*, affords him; the Power of the Confederacy againft him may be broken, by difuniting the Confederat s. Hiftory fatisfies us how feldom a Confederacy of many Princes, has ever ruined a fingle Power attacked. I have given one Inftance of this already, when I fpoke of the Grand Alliance againft *Lewis* XIV. and the League of *Cambray* againft the *Venetians*, in the 16th Century, is an Inftance ftill more remarkable.

But, if contrary to our Hopes, our Wifhes, our Endeavours, this fhould fail; if his *Pruffian* Majefty, like a Lion caught in the Toils (after a Refiftance already made, which will hand him down to Pofterity as the greateft of Men) fhould at laft be unable to defend himfelf; let him not defpair while he is in Alliance with *Britain*: For I would inculcate a Doctrine, which I th nk will not be

unpopular

4

unpopular amongſt my Countrymen, and which, therefore, I hope, will not be oppoſed by our Mi- niſters, *That whatever Conqueſts we have made, and whatever Conqueſts we may ſtill make, upon the* French, *except* North America, *which muſt be kept all our own* ; *ſhould be looked upon as given back to* France *for a moſt important Conſideration, if it can be the Means of extricating the King of* Pruſſia *from any unforeſeen Diſtreſſes.*

Perhaps my Notions on this Subject may ſeem to border on Enthuſiaſm; but, however, I can- not but be perſuaded, that Things are come to that Paſs in *Germany*, that the Ruin of the King of *Pruſſia* will be ſoon followed by the Ruin of the Proteſtant Religion in the Empire The blind Zeal of the bigotted *Auſtrian* Family will have no Check, if the Head and Protector of the *German* Prote- ſtants be deſtroyed ; and the War begun only to wreſt *Sileſia* from him, will, in the End, be found to be a War that will overturn the Liberties and Religion of *Germany*. If, therefore, the noble Perſeverance of the King of *Pruſſia* deſerves the Eſteem of a generous People ; if his Fidelity to his Engagements, which has contributed to ſave *Hanover* and to ruin *France*, can demand our Gra- titude ; if the Danger of the only Proteſtant So- vereign in *Germany*, able to preſerve the Privileges of his Religion from being trampled under Foot, can call forth the warm Support of this Proteſtant Nation ; may I not hope, may I not be confident, that our Miniſters will dictate, and our People approve of Terms of Peace in his Favour, tho' they ſhould be purchaſed by relinquiſhing ſome of our Conqueſts; while the Poſſeſſion of *Canada* will be ſo reaſonable a Bound to the Demands we may make for ourſelves ?

I

I have stated this Point, upon a Suppolition that the Event of the War may turn out to the Difadvantage of the King of *Pruffia*. But if the Fortune, the Capacity, the Perfeverance of that Great Prince, fhould enable him (as I think we may ftill hope) to extricate himfelf from the Dangers that furround him——it may be afked, What is to be done with the Conquefts which, befides *Canada*, we fhall be in Poffeffion of when we treat of a Peace?——My Propofal is honeft, and perhaps will not be treated as chimerical : Employ them to recover out of the Hands of *France* thofe Towns of *Flanders*, gained for the *Auftrian* Family by the Valour, and at the Expence of *England*; and which have been fo perfidioufly facrificed. A *Britifh* Adminiftration muft tremble at the Profpect of feeing *Newport* and *Oftend* become *French* Property, and, therefore, fhould ufe their utmoft Endeavours to prevent this at the Peace ; tho' thofe Endeavours may ferve the Court of *Vienna*, whofe Ingratitude to *Britain* never will be forgotten ; tho', at the fame Time, I muft own we fhall draw no fmall Advantage from it. We fhall learn, for the future, to prefer our own Intereft to that of others ; to proportion our Expences on the Continent to the immediate Exigencies of our own Country, and never to affift a *new* Ally, without remembering how much we did for our Old one, and what Return we have had !

I have, now, nearly executed my principal Defign, in the prefent Addrefs ; which was to give my Thoughts on the important Bufinefs of the approaching Treaty. And if it be conducted with as much Ability, as the War has been carried on with Spirit and Succefs, there is great Room for flattering ourfelves, that the Voice of the Publick demands no Advantages or Ceffions, in Favour of

Eng-

England, which the Minifters of *England* are not refolved to infift upon.

But amidft the fignal Succeffes of our Arms, which give us fo reafonable an Expectation of an honourable Peace, and have exalted our Country to the higheft Pinnacle of Glory and Reputation abroad—I wifh it could be faid that our *Conftitution* was not greatly in Danger of being hurt, and almoft loft, at *Home*.—I fhall beg Leave to take this Occafion of touching this equally melancholy and important Subject; with a View, not to blame, but to lament; not to bring any railing Accufation againft thofe who are now in Power, but to exhort and to excite them to endeavour, before it be too late, to add to the Services they have done their Country, in faving it from the open Attacks of *France*, the ftill more important Service of faving our Confti tution, which fome unhappy Circumftances of our prefent Situation have already greatly changed, and feem to threaten with intire Deftruction;—Nay, I may fay, would have actually deftroyed, if it were not for the good Heart of our gracious Sovereign, who fcorns to take Advantage of them.

Confiderably above an hundred Millions of Debt, the Sum we muft be obliged to fit down with, at the End of the prefent War, is a Burthen which, however immenfe, Experience has taught us, contrary to all Theory, we fhall be able to bear without *Bankruptcy*. As our Expences have increafed, we have found, contrary to the Predictions of gloomy Politicians, that our Abilities to bear them have increafed alfo.—But tho' our Debts be not too great for the Riches of our Country, they are much too great for the Independency of its Conftitution. For, when I confider the infinite Dependance upon the Crown, created by Means of Them, throughout the Kingdom, amongft all Degrees of

Men;

Men; when I reflect on the many Thousands of Placemen, of every Denomination, who are employed in the Collection of the vast Variety of Taxes now levied on the Public; and take a Review of a far greater Number of Servants of the Crown, both Civil and Military, for whose Support so considerable a Share of the public Revenue is set apart, too many of whom, I fear, might be tempted to assist in extending the Influence of the Prerogative to the Prejudice of public Liberty; when I consider our vast Load of Taxes, in this Point of View, I cannot help observing the amazing Revolution in our Government which this single *Article* has brought about; nor enough lament the unhappy Circumstances of Affairs, and the Necessities of the War which have forced us to an annual Expence, unknown to former Times, and which will almost be incredible to Posterity. I believe I can venture to say upon Memory, that the Expences of the War, for all King *William*'s Reign, about 13 Years, were not, at a Medium, above 3 Millions and a half a Year; and Queen *Anne*'s, tho' the last Years were exorbitant, were little more than 5 Millions. What they are *now* I sigh to think on. Twelve or Fourteen Millions are demanded without Reserve; and, what is still more, voted without Opposition. Nay, of so little Consequence is it now thought, by our Representatives, to deliberate on the weighty Business of raising Money on the Subject, that scarcely can *Forty* of them be got together, to hear the Estimates for at least *One hundred and fourscore Thousand* Men, for so many we have now in our Pay; and to borrow *Eight Millions*, the Sum by which our Expences exceed our Income.

These are alarming Considerations; but another Object, no less threatening the Ruin of our Constitution, also presents itself.

I am

I am old enough to remember what Uneafinefs and Jealoufies difturbed the Minds of all true Patriots, with regard to ftanding Armies, and military Eftablifhments. Principles of Liberty in general, and, in particular, Whig Principles, excited this Uneafinefs and produced thofe Jealoufies, which, from Time to Time, have been a fruitful Source of Parliamentary Debate. It was no longer ago than the late King's Time, that the vefting *Courts Martial*, in Time of Peace, with the Power of punifhing *Mutiny* and *Defertion* with *Death*, was carried in the Houfe of Commons by a fmall Majority *. Nay, that a Court Martial, however limited in its Jurisdiction, was inconfiftent with the Liberties of a free People, in Time of Peace, was the Doctrine of Whigs in thofe Days ; it was the Doctrine, in particular, of Sir *Robert Walpole* then in Oppofition ; whofe remarkable Expreffion, in this great Debate, " That they who gave the *Power of Blood, gave Blood,*" never can be forgotten. And though afterwards when he came to be a *Minifter*, he was better reconciled to ftanding Armies and Mutiny Bills, in Time of Peace, *feventeen* thoufand Men, was all the Army he *durft* afk; yet even that Demand produced an *annual* Debate ; and the *annual* Reafon, on which he founded the Neceffity of his Demand — being the Danger from the Pretender and the Jacobites; was the ftrongeft Proof, that even in Sir *R. Walpole*'s Opinion, the Reduction in the Army fhould take Place, when this Danger from Difaffection fhould ceafe. But how are Things changed ? — I own indeed that amidft the Dangers of this War, and the Threats of an Invafion, the vaft Army now on our Efta-

---

* In 1717-18 the Numbers on the Divifion were 247 to 229.

blifh-

blifhment, is neceffary : But what I lament is to
fee the Sentiments of the Nation fo amazingly reconciled to the Profpect of having a far more numerous Body of regular Troops, kept up, after
the Peace, than any true Lover of his Country in
former Times thought, could be allowed without
endangering the Conftitution.   Nay, fo unaccount-
ably fond are we become of the military Plan,
that the Erection of Barracks, which, twenty Years
ago, would have ruined any Minifter who fhould
have ventured to propofe it, may be propofed fafe-
ly by our Minifters now a-Days and, upon Trial,
be found to be a favourite Meafure with our Patriots, and with the Public in general.

But what I lament as the greateft Misfortune
that can threaten the public Liberty, is to fee the
Eagernefs with which our Nobility, born to be the
Guardians of the Conftitution againft Prerogative,
folicit the Badge of *military* Subjection, not merely
to ferve their Country, in Times of Danger, which
would be commendable, but in Expectation to be
continued *Soldiers*, when Tranquillity fhall be reftored, and to be under *military Command*, during
Life.   When I fee this ftrange, but melancholy
Infatuation, fo prevalent, I almoft defpair of the
Conftitution.   If it fhould go on in Proportion as
it has of late, I fear the Time will, at laft, come,
when Independence on the Crown, will be exploded
as unfafhionable.   Unlefs another Spirit poffefs our
Nobility ; unlefs they lay afide their Military Trap-
pings ; and think they they can ferve their Country more effectually as Senators than as Soldiers,
what can we expect but to fee, the Syftem of military Subordination extending itfelf throughout the
Kingdam, univerfal Dependance upon Government
nfluencing every Rank of Men, and the Spirit,

nay

nay the very Form of the Conftitution deftroyed ?
We have generally beaten the *French*, and always
been foolifh enough to follow their Fafhions; 1 was
in Hopes we fhould never have taken the Fafhion
of *French* Government ; but from our numerous
Armies, and the military Turn of our Nobility, I
am afraid we are running into it as faft as we can.
And, unlefs fomething can be done, to bring back
our Conftitution to its firft Principles, we fhall find,
that we have triumphed, only to make ourfelves
as wretched as our Enemy; that our Conquefts are
but a poor Compenfation for the Lofs of our Liberties; in a Word, that, like *Wolfe*, falling in the
Arms of Victory, we are moft glorioufly—*undone!*

But though I have drawn fo melancholy a Pic-
ture, of the Dangers which threaten us with the
Lofs of our Liberties, it is with no other Defign,
than to exhort thofe who are placed at the Helm,
to fet about the Repairs of our fhattered Veffel,
as foon as fhe can be brought fafe into Harbour. After the Peace is once fettled, it ought to
be the great Object of our Minifters, to devife
every Expedient, and to adopt every Plan, that
may extricate this unhappy Conftitution from the
Dangers I have defcribed. Confidering the low
Ebb of *France*, we have fome Reafon to hope that
when Peace is once reftored, upon folid Terms, it
will not foon be interrupted. Much, therefore,
may be done during thofe Years of Tranquility;
if our Minifters be diligent and faithful in this
great Work of reviving the Conftitution. The
facred, and inviolable Application of the *Sinking
Fund*, which the Increafe of our Trade, and other
Circumftances, have fo greatly augmented, and
muft ftill augment, will operate gradually, and effectually. Univerfal and invariable Œconomy,
muft

muſt be introduced into every Branch of Government ; the Revenues of the Kingdom may be
vaſtly increaſed by adopting Schemes that will prevent Frauds, and leſſen the Expence of Collection ; innumerable unneceſſary Places may be abo-
liſhed, and exorbitant Perquiſites, in thoſe we leave,
may be reſtrained ; Attention muſt be had to the
Morals and Principles of the Nation, and the Revival
of Virtue and of Religion will go hand in hand,
with the Revival of Liberty. But no Object will
deſerve more Attention, than our Military Encroachments on Conſtitutional Independance.
When this War ſhall be over, there will be leſs
Reaſon, than ever, for numerous Armies. The
Kingdom now happily being united, and Diſaffec-
tion to the Royal Family at an End, we need fear
no Rebellions among ourſelves ; and Invaſions from
France are leſs likely than ever. Beſides, by the
Care and Perſeverance of ſome Patriots, we have
acquired a new internal Strength, a Militia trained
up to be uſeful, and conſequently, we may without
any Danger to the Public, reduce the Number of
our Guards and Garriſons, ſo low, as to deſtroy
great Part of the huge Fabrick of Military Influence and Dependance. But whatever you do, if
you mean to reſtore the Conſtitution, you muſt
ſecure the Dignity and Independance of Parliament.
After paſſing ſuch Laws as may ſtill be neceſſary to
preſerve the Freedom of Elections, from Influence
of every Sort ; to puniſh Bribery both in the *Elec-
tors* and in the *Elected*; ſomething, perhaps, may
ſtill be done by Way of Place-bill, to leſſen mini-
ſterial Influence over Parliaments, without having
Recourſe to an *Oliverian* Self-*denying* Ordinance ;
or to ſo total an Excluſion of Placemen as was
eſtabliſhed, in the original Act of Settlement.

And.

And an Houfe of Commons thus chofen, and thus made independent, now that *Jacobitifm* is rooted out, can never be formidable but to thofe who have Reafon to tremble. Such an Houfe of Commons, will co-operate with the Adminiftration in every Plan of publick Utility, and at the fame Time inquire carefully into the Abufes of Government; Supplies will be voted; but only in Proportion to the real Income and Abilities of the Nation; and we may expect to fee, what we have not feen above thefe foity Years, a Parliamentary Commiffion of Accounts erected to inquire into the Difburfement of near *Two Hundred Millions.* And unlefs we fee this, foon, I fhall look upon our Conftitution, as loft, for ever.

Thefe, and many fuch Regulations, as thefe, may, under an honeft and virtuous Adminiftration, be adopted when once Peace is reftored: And the Profpect of feeing them adopted, and fteadily purfued, keeps me from defpairing altogether of the *Commonwealth.*

To you, therefore, whofe Power, moft likely, will not terminate with the War; and whom I have prefumed to addrefs, with Regard to the Terms that fhould be demanded, to fecure us from a perfidious Foe; To you, *My Lord,* and *Sir,* let me earneftly recommend, the ftill more important Care, of faving us, from *ourfelves*; and as you have with an Unanimity, that doth you both great Honour, directed our Councils, fo as to humble *France,* let me intreat you to preferve your Union, till it re-invigorate the almoft loft Powers of the *Britifh Conftitution.*

If you have any Regard to Virtue, to Liberty, to your Country; if you would live great, and die lamented; if you would fhine in Hiftory, with our

H   *Clarendons*

Clarendons and *Southamptons*; let not this Opportunity, perhaps, this laſt Opportunity of ſaving *Britiſh* Liberty, and Independence, be thrown away. You, *my Lord*, whoſe Rank, whoſe extenſive Influence, and perſonal Authority, have given you the Preeminence, in public Affairs, as it were by Preſcription; much will depend upon you, in the carrying on this important Work. But when I direct my Addreſs to you, *Sir*, you muſt be conſcious that beſides the general Expectations we have from you, as a Lover of Your Country, we have your own repeated Promiſes, and Declarations, to make us flatter ourſelves that you will not ſtop ſhort, in your Schemes of national Reformation. Not tutored in the School of Corruption, but liſted, from your earlieſt Years, under the Banner of Patriotiſm; called into Power, by popular Approbation, and ſtill uniting, the uncommon Characters of *Miniſter* and *Patriot*; favourite of the Public, and Servant of the Crown; be not offended, Sir, if I remind you, not to Diſappoint that Confidence the Public places in your future Endeavours to prop the ſinking Conſtitution. Nor let it ever fall from your Memory, that the Nation expects from your Virtue, your Œconomy, your Plans for Liberty, during the future Peace, as great Advantages as we have already gained, from your Spirit, your bold Councils, and vigorous Efforts, in carrying on the preſent War.

Perhaps I grow too warm, on a favorite Subject; and, therefore, from Schemes which cannot take Effect, till the War be cloſed, let me turn your Attention again, for a little while longer, to the Object immediately before our Eyes----the inſuing Conferences for Peace. And, with Regard to theſe, though I ſuppoſe, they will *begin*, before
the

the Winter be 'over, I think there is fome Reafon, for be ng of Opinion that we muft have another Campaign, before they can be finally clofed. *France* is too low, to think ferioufly of a Peace, without making fome defperate Effort. She never would have expof.d her Weaknefs to all *Europe*, by fo fhameful and fo humbling a Bankruptcy ; She never would have ruined her public Credit, and melted her Plate, the laft Refource, when every other ha, been exhaufted, only to receive Terms from *England*. No, fhe knows fhe is un-done, for ever, if fhe gets no footing in *Hanover* ; and, therefore, we may expect to fee another At-tempt made for that Purpofe. But, if we are not wanting to ourfelves, another Attempt, will end, as unfortunately for her, as the former have done ; and her Ruin only be more confirmed. In the mean while, I make no Doubt, the Plenipotentiaries will meet at a Congrefs ; but the Events of the Field, muft regulate the Deliberations of the Cabinet. We, no Doubt, fhall be *firm* in our Demands, *whatever they are* ; and the *French* will endeavour to gain Time, to know whether there is any likeli-hood of obliging us to offer them *better*. In this Situation, then, *France* muft hear with Terror, that without breaking our national Faith, without injuring private Property, without giving exorbi-tant Premiums, we have already provided *immenfely* for the Supplies of *another* Year (and Supplies for *Years* may ftill be had) to meet them--not in *Ame-rita* ; there they are no more ;—not on the *Ocean*---the Deftruction of their Fleets leaves that Empire free to us--but once more, on the Plains of another *Minden*, again to feel and to confefs the Superiority of *Britifh* Valour.

H 2

I have

I have only a Particular or two, to add, before I conclude. And I cannot help congratulating the Public, on the Wisdom of our Manner of Opening the Negociation for Peace. I mean to obferve, that our Minifters have happily got rid of a Set of very *ufelefs*, or very *pernicious* Gentlemen called *Mediators*, by applying directly to the Enemy himfelf. Nothing can be more ridiculous than the Figure of the *Pope's* Nuncio, and the Ambaffador of *Venice*, acting the Farce of Mediation at *Munfter*, for feveral Years, while the War went on, till its Events regulated the Terms of Peace. The Mediation of *infignificant* Powers is therefore abfurd ; and the Danger of calling in a *powerful* Mediator, who may threaten to declare againft you, if you do not fubmit to his *partial* Decifions, is too obvious to be infifted upon. You have done wifely, therefore, to keep the Negociation in your own Hands ; the Nation, from this Inftance, has a full Confidence that her Interefts, are fkilfully conducted; and, therefore, I fhall only add, another Particular, which however fubordinate, will, no Doubt be attended to by you ; though *fome late* Negotiators of ours, with *France*, neglected it.

The *French*, by taking the Lead in *Europe* of late, have, of Courfe, been able to introduce their Language as the common Vehicle of the Sentiments of other Nations, in all public Negociations ; fo that, perhaps, the *French* is the only Tongue, by the Chanel of which Plenipotentiaries and Minifters of different Countries, can converfe. But when the Negociation is to be put into Writing, and to be drawn up in that Form which is to be binding upon all the Parties, and figned jointly by the treating Powers, neither the Honour, nor the Intereft of the State, ought to allow us, to accept

of

of the Original Treaty in the *Native Tongue* of our
Enemies.   The Honour of the Nation forbids this;
as it would be a Confeffion of Superiority, to which
Britain, at no Time, much lefs after fo glorious a
War, fhould fubmit ; efpecially as we cannot fubmit to it, without giving the Enemy a real Ad-
vantage, and laying the Foundation for future
Cavils.—Cardinal *Mazarine*, in his Letters, boafts,
that by a latent Ambiguity and Nicety in the *French*
Stile, he had been able to out-wit *Don Louis de
Haro*, in the Conferences at the *Pyrenees*.   And a
much later Inftance, in which we ourfelves were
partly concerned, fhould confirm us, in our Refu-
fal to treat with the *French* in their own Language.
—I mean the famous Capitulation of the *Dutch*
Garrifon of *Tournay* in 1745; which, though only
reftrained from acting, for a limited Time in any
of the Barrier Towns *, as the *Dutch* believed,
when they accepted of the Capitulation, was foon
after interpreted by *France*, as tying them up from
acting in any Part of the World ; and might have
been fatal to this Country, if the Rebellion in *Scot-
land*, to affift in quelling which the *Dutch* lent us
thofe very Troops, had been fo fuccefsful, as to
oblige us to put our Foreign Allies to the Teft.

We have no great Reafon, no more than other
Nations, to truft *Gallic Faith*, as appears from the
many Inftances of their *unpalliated* Perfidy which I
have collected above.   Let us not, therefore, be

* I have not the original Capitulation before me, but I
remember, pretty exactly on what the Cavil turned.   The
Troops were not to act, I think, for two Years, in any of the
Places *les plus reculées de le Barriere*.   The *Dutch*, no doubt, underftood, *de la Barriere* to be the *Genitive* Cafe, but the *French*
faid they meant it in the *Ablative*.

fo

so weak as to give them Room for obtruding upon us, any fallacious Interpretations of the Words, in which they plight their Faith. They are too ready to break it when the Terms are ever so clear ; and, therefore, let us take Care not to give them that Advantage which superior Skill in their own Language, naturally confers, and which upon some future Occasion, they may improve to our Detriment. Let the *original and authentic* Copy of the Treaty, therefore be in a dead Language, the Phrases of which cannot vary, and whose Meaning is equally understood by both Parties. We had once a very learned Plenipotentiary in Queen *Elizabeth*'s Time, who, in a Negociation with *Spain*, when it came to be debated in what Language the Treaty should be made, ludricously enough proposed to the *Spaniard*, who was giving himself Airs of Superiority, to treat in the Language of his Master's Kingdom of *Jerusalem*. But leaving the *Hebrew*, for our Divines ; I would only have our Negociators treat in *Latin:* Which seemed, as it were by Prescription, to have a Right to be the Language of the Public Law of *Europe*; till some late Instances have shewn that the *French* was beginning to be substituted in its Room ; by the Laziness or Neglect of those who treated. As we are sanguine in our Hopes of a much better Peace than we had at *Utrecht*, with Regard to the Terms ; let it not, be worse than that at *Utrecht*, which preserved the Old Custom of settling the Negociation in *Latin*. We then had a Bishop indeed, as Plenipotentiary; but without having Recourse to the very learned Bench, or choosing a Plenipotentiary from *Cambridge* (I hope in a little Time one may join the other University, without giving Offence) the Negociators at the ensuing fuing Peace, may be accommodated with *Latin* enough for the Purpofe I mention, at a very moderate Expence—if their Secretary or Chaplain cannot affift them.

But when I begin to be ludicrous on fo ferious a Subject, it is Time to have done : And my Addrefs has already fwelled to fuch a fize as furprizes myfelf, as much, as I fear it will tire the Reader. However, the vaft Variety of Facts, and Particulars, which naturally offered themfelves to me, and which could not be omitted without hurting the Connexion, and weakening my Argument, will, perhaps, procure Indulgence for fo long a Pamphlet : And, for the fame Reafon, I flatter myfelf, that if I fhould happen to have been miftaken in any Thing I advance, to have erred in a Date, or to have mif-quoted a Treaty, fome Allowances will be made to me, as I have been obliged to truft much to my Memory, for want of a proper Opportunity of confulting many of thofe Books, which furnifh the Materials I have made Ufe of. However, I believe a candid Reader, will find no *capital*, at leaft, no *wilful*, Miftake.

I am far from the Vanity of thinking that my Notions on the important Subject of the Peace, are a regular Plan or Syftem for the Adminiftration to proceed upon. I throw them out, only as loofe Hints for my *Superiors* to improve as they may think proper. Should there be any Weight in all, or any of them, you, *my Lord* and *Sir*, will be able to work them into Utility for this Kingdom. If they are not worth your Notice ; as I am an anonymous Writer, and hope never to be known, I can neither lofe nor gain Reputation

by